A Kingdom of Queens

A Kingdom of Queens copyright © 2019 by Hannah E Baldwin.

Illustrations copyright © 2019 by Chloe Bailey

Illustrations copyright © 2019 by Charlotte Smith

Illustrations copyright © 2019 by Olivia Pinnock

ISBN: 9781798924723

Acknowledgments

Thanks to all the women who inspired me to write these poems and thanks to Jordan for getting bored of hearing them and encouraging me to share them with the world.

Women don't need your validation
Or your derogatory remarks, with your
Mediocre deception.
End your
Narrow frame of mind.

All we need is to be listened to.
Reminder: we are humans too,
Even without a cock.

Women aren't just mothers,
Or cleaners, or cooks.
No!
Don't complain about the noise we make
Early in the morning as we're preparing your lunch
Ready for you to go to work, before we go to the office too.
For we are just being kind.
Unknown ideas we have deserve to be validated.
Listen: women just want to be heard.

here we are

waiting to be

d

r

o

w

n

e

d

for our sins.

but what are our sins?

~ helping others is not a form of witchcraft ~

signs that you might be a witch:

knowledge can be your kryptonite
you just have a hunch and
nature feels natural

you honour and respect boundaries
are perceptive and attentive
and are born to keep secrets

you want to help
and heal
and grow

~ does being a witch really sound so bad? ~

summon the darkness

summon the light

summon every woman

who has met persecution

        let us burn

        let us heal

        let us grow

        let us be

        ~ we can rise against this, together ~

    b r e a k me

i dare you

    set me on

f i r e

    and like a phoenix i will

            e

        s

    i

 r

just to prove you wrong

    ~ show them that you're strong ~

one of our biggest fears

is the pressure to be

           p r e t t y

one of our biggest fears

is the pressure to be

           s k i n n y

one of our biggest fears

is the pressure to fall in

           l o v e

with someone who won't let

us feel

           c o n t r o l

of ourselves

        ~ pressure is now our biggest fear ~

i've opened my eyes

and my mind is full of fear

because i'm feeling

~ emotions aren't as scary as you think ~

we're promiscuous,

our hands are great at manipulating

  s m a l l somethings.

we have mental whiskers,

to sense menace,

from aggressive men and

repression.

~ women are just like red squirrels ~

there's buzzing in the room next door

it's been vibrating for almost half an hour

i wonder what setting she has it on

it sounds like it's changing pace

i wonder if i should go and tell her

that this is simply not acceptable

~ i hope she found a climax ~

can you hear me scream

can you hear me scream your name

please don't fucking stop

                 ~ we can be in control too ~

send nudes

my dudes

and by nudes

i mean lipstick swatches

~ everyone suits a nude ~

jhmdfgsdfesxazxc

htuyfgs xdnm

jhfgfryk,jhcxwefgbbfg

~ some advice from my cat* ~

* yes, he did type this himself

when do you want to find a boyfriend?

when do you want to get married?

when do you want to have kids?

when do you want to find a job?

why don't you have a boyfriend?

why aren't you married?

why haven't you had kids?

why haven't you found a better job?

how is the boyfriend?

how is the wedding planning?

how are the kids?

how is the new job?

~ some questions feel like burdens ~

but it's better now

you definitely get paid the same

feminists are crazy

we're all equal

hello sir could you lift this box

sorry ma'am, do you know where i can get this dry cleaned

would you ask these questions

the other way around

~ i thought feminism was more accessible ~

we are not equal

patriarchy is still real

we are so foolish

~ but we're going to keep trying ~

surround yourself

with supportive women

because you never know

when you may need their

        ((protection))

~ they'll protect you when the bad parts of life bite ~

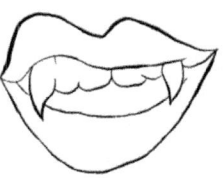

i always feel conscious

of my little pooch

but she cushions some of

my important bits

she can protect my ovaries

and my babies

so really we should thank her

for her help

rather than trying to

flatten her out

~ thank your little pooch – she's just trying to do her job ~

sometimes it takes loving

someone else's flaws to

                learn

what it takes to love

          yourself

      ~ fall in love with your own flaws too ~

i want to

walk the night

without being afraid

of what or who is

                        hiding

behind every corner

       ~ i shouldn't be scared for my own safety ~

sometimes the only

 comfort

we can find is from

 food

which is not a healthy

 relationship

but i can rely on food more

 than any man

~ form secure relationships with other humans not food ~

women who inspire me

charlotte, my dear,

you always know the right things to say,

and i must make it clear,

i just can't stay away.

your kind heart brings everyone joy,

your shoes are the best in the room,

honestly, you're the best boy,

you make my spirit bloom.

charlotte, my dear,

i think you underestimate,

what you do to my cerebral hemisphere*,

and honestly, your tits are pretty great.

my sonnet ends here today,

it already looks a bit like literature essay

* each of the two parts of the cerebrum** (left and right) in the brain of a vertebrate.

**it is responsible for the integration of complex sensory and neural functions and the initiation and coordination of voluntary activity in the body.

~ this is a bit silly but thank you for always encouraging me ~

my happy little trio

that i will never take for granted

two of the strongest women

in the world to me

with their own stories to tell.

one is off to america

to kickstart part of her career

i will always support her

but god i'll miss her

for the summer she is gone.

one is a process operator*

which sounds like something

only a man would do

but she's better at it

than any of the men

because she can do it with nail extensions.

these women i have known since we were

just girls

we've been together

and a p a r t

but these 12 years off friendship

will always be in my heart.

a support system

a bitching session

a whole decade of inside jokes.

a group chat that's on fire

a blonde, a brunette, and a ginger -

together we can take on the world.

* she oversees and manages the full production process of a gas terminal - she monitors equipment to ensure the quality, efficiency and safety of the plant.

~ thank you for always keeping me on track ~

my best friend is fierce,

my best friend is kind,

my best friend doesn't know about this poem,

but hopefully she doesn't mind.

although somedays can be a struggle for her,

i know she will never give up trying,

to better herself and study for her career,

which is something i will always admire.

she has a brain like nobody i know,

she can analyse and compare every

bit of prose (and hopefully this poem).

she has the reading speed of a jaguar

and a brain so full of realms,

the imagination of a child,

sometimes i am surprised she's not overwhelmed.

i know she will always support me,

even when i send her my crazy ideas,

about silly stories and character conspiracies,

and she's still trying to work with me to get over one of my fears.

(it's snakes and she is the fucking reptile queen).

we've agreed to grow old,

and move to a far away forest,

without our boyfriends,

to ever bother us.

we're going to take all of our pets,

because they're always going to be with us,

and honestly, clo,

i cant wait until the kids think we're witches.

~ thanks for always giving me the best book recs ~

honestly, mum, you drive me insane,

you're a bloody lunatic,

but i've never been so glad to have a

woman

like you around

you always inspire me,

you love every part of me,

even when i don't know how to love

myself

i'm lucky to have you, mum,

and it's something i take for granted too often.

to have constant support,

with whatever i do

(even if it means moving all of my shit across the country)

and you're pretty damn sexy for an oldie too.

so i guess this is thank you for all the times i haven't said it,

thank you for raising me to do what i love,

thank you for raising me - full stop.

~ i don't know what i did for a mum like you but thank you ~

just a couple left now

Uy7yu68inh

~ another piece of advice by a different cat ~

sisters not twins

but wait

they're not even

one is fatter

now this one is a different angle

one is darker

i just cant win

maybe i'll start over

        ~ you were beautiful from the beginning ~

badass females aren't only found in books

be your own protagonist

not your own villain

~ you're a badass female too ~

Notes:

Printed in Great Britain
by Amazon